❝ The soil produces everything we possess. ❞

Mr Middleton, 1945

❝ Until I got involved with SHEDx I had no idea how much history of growing there was in the area. It has got me really excited about what is here. ❞

SHEDx volunteer, 2019

Introduction 3

The Beginning 5

The Good Life 14

The Growing Community 22

Change of Land Use 29

The Shed 41

The Heritage Shed 46

Allotment Holders Tales 55

Growing Ideas in Tolworth 67

'SHEDx – Grow for Good' celebrates the history of allotments in Tolworth, Surbiton and Chessington in the London borough of Kingston upon Thames. This book captures some of the projects research and findings and we are grateful to all the volunteers who helped bring 'SHEDx – Grow for Good' alive. We are particularly grateful to The National Lottery Heritage Fund for their support and assistance.

'SHEDx – Grow for Good' helped to stimulate a much larger programme 'SHEDx – Growing Ideas in Tolworth' which is supported by the Mayor of London and the Royal Borough of Kingston upon Thames. This project is aimed at encouraging local communities to help guide the regeneration and greening of the area.

SHEDx - Grow for Good
The Beginning

" The soil produces everything we possess. "

Mr Middleton, 1945

In Britain today around 300,000 people have an allotment. They are deeply associated with quintessential British life and conjure up notions of nostalgia, tranquility and a simpler life. Having one's own plot of land gives growers a sense of independence and this strong relationship with the land runs deeply in the character of the nation. History is full of examples of land struggles, such as those of the Diggers, who in 1649 took claim to common lands in places such as Weybridge in Surrey, in order to cultivate crops, declaring that using the earth would enable true freedom.

Yet, in a stark contrast to the romantic notions, the allotment was actually born out of dire poverty. The Agricultural Depression of the 1880s hit labourers across the country hard, so landowners, who could not afford to pay them more, provided them with allotments to prevent starvation. They were a necessary burden and one which added to their already gruelling worklife, a point of great contention. In 1884, when labourers won the right to vote, they were such an important issue that the 1889 election was nicknamed the "allotment elections".

At the start of the 19th Century the use of allotments to alleviate hunger and financial hardship began to spread to the towns and cities where urban poverty was a growing concern. Some of the more forward-thinking factory owners and railway companies were providing their employees with land to grow their own food, but the problem was widespread. Chocolatier and social reformer Joseph Rowntree created 4000 plots for his employees as a result of a survey undertaken by his family in 1901, which found 1 in 5 of the population of York had less food than the inmates of the workhouse or prison.

The district of Surbiton, located in north Surrey, alongside the bustling and historic market town of Kingston upon Thames, was a relatively new urban area with rural parts to the south. Though not battling the poverty of industrial cities, at the turn of the century it already had some allotment provision, such as on Lord Lovelace's land in Tolworth, but not enough to meet demand. In 1908 the government passed the Smallholdings and Allotment Act, which for the first time required local councils to set aside land for allotments. In January of that year, Surbiton Urban District Council had already received a petition from 10 allotment holders asking for land to be provided under the new act, and so that spring the Recreation Grounds and Allotments Committee began to look at the purchase of land for allotments at Tolworth and Red Lion Field, as well as other potential sites.

Every aspect of British life was affected by the World Wars, and the allotments were no exception. Though many are familiar with the Second World War Dig for Victory campaign, during the First World War an unexpected combination of poor harvests and decreasing imports in 1917 created a critical food shortage and prompted the first movement to get Britain growing its own food.

On the outbreak of war in 1914, Surbiton showed no concern about threats to food supplies for its residents. While tensions grew in Europe, the Recreation Grounds and Allotments Committee were occupied discussing local issues, such as the damage caused to the flowers on Mr J C Upton's allotment borders. It wasn't until late 1915 that Surrey County Council started to encourage people to grow more food and established the County War Agricultural Committee. They asked Surbiton to consider forming a similar committee and support this movement, which was decided against. It took another year and encouragement by the Board of Agriculture for the council to change their mind, when they began looking at potential allotment sites and accepting applications from landowners. However, progress was slow and in February 1917 a further request to form a committee by the County War Agricultural Committee was still met with opposition by officials.

It would appear the establishment of war time allotments was embraced more enthusiastically elsewhere in Britain, with the overall national response to the worsening food crisis seen to be highly impressive. Even George V turned the flower beds outside Buckingham Palace over for use for food crops and the Archbishop of Canterbury sanctioned work on Sundays for Christians to help support the movement which became known as the "Garden Front".

Surbiton had mixed success in securing new plots. The committee did not feel that breaking up recreation grounds in populated areas would be of any benefit and so were trying to secure private land instead. Some landowners were happy to give their land over for an annual fee, and others, such as the owners of Regent House, decided to cultivate the land themselves. However, some showed resistance including a Mrs Cundy who, despite negotiations with the council, was not prepared to let any of her land at Seething Wells. She later did offer some land in Southborough Park, but it is unclear from the minutes as to whether the details were agreed on before peace was declared.

The national impact on allotments during the First World War was huge and the number of plots in Britain grew from 450,000 to 1.5 million. With peace there was, as expected, a gradual decline in the number of plots, but mass demobilisation, efforts to give plots to returning soldiers, the closure of munitions factories, and then the depression of the 1920s meant many people continued to rely on their allotments as a stable food source.

However, it was not long before Europe was back on the brink of war and plans began to be made for food rationing and the revival of a campaign to grow. Alongside this, the government hoped that more home grown food would help alleviate concerns around potential recruits, as working class soldiers in both the Boer and First World War were often malnourished and suffered from poor health.

❝ It is clearly our duty...to try and make doubly and trebly sure that we will fight and win this war on full stomachs... ❞

Sir Reginald Dorman-Smith,
Minister for Agriculture, 3 October 1939

Tolworth Infants & Junior School playing fields allotments, 1946

Despite the planning, Britain went to war with just 4 months of food in stock and immediately passed the Cultivation of Lands (Allotments) Order 1939, allowing local councils to take over unoccupied land and open up temporary allotments whenever possible. Unlike with the previous war, this time Surbiton jumped into action and in September 1939 at a Town Council meeting it was agreed that the Borough Surveyor and Chairman of the Allotments Sub-Committee would survey the borough for possible new allotment sites immediately. Some residents were eager to offer up land, such as Miss Wilson of 7 Woodlands Road who offered land at the rear of numerous properties on that road as "owing to physical disability I personally am unable to undertake work of National Importance, though able to carry on in business, I feel I should like to do something to help the Nation…"

In other circumstances, the borough got a little over enthusiastic in trying to secure land for allotments, and after trying to acquire land from Prewitt's Dairies on Hampton Hill, received a response which stated: "I fully appreciate that your committee wish during the period of war to make the best production from the ground mentioned, but fail to see any better use other than at present adopted, viz: the grazing of milking cows for the production of milk, can be of greater benefit to the nation."

HOOK WILL HAVE FLOWER SHOW

Society to Support Grow More Food Campaign

Hook and District Horticultural Society is to carry on its work in the district during the war and to give its support to the campaign to grow more food.

This was agreed unanimously at the society's annual meeting at the North Star, Hook, on Wednesday, when it was also decided to hold the annual show on July 24.

Alderman P. W. Rampton was elected president, in succession to Mr. J. Ramsay Kerby, who had held that position for nearly 20 years.

After paying tribute to Mr. Ramsay Kerby's work for the society Mr. C. R. Kitson (hon. secretary) reviewed what he described as a disturbed year. Although the weather affected the annual show, the quality of the exhibits was up to the usual high standard. The sports organised by Mr. J. H. Wade, were an outstanding success. Mr. Kitson wished good luck to members of the society serving with the Forces and hoped that they would have a speedy return.

Mr. H. W. Edwards (hon. treasurer) presented the accounts, which showed that the year began with a balance in hand of £19 13s. 4d., subscriptions and donations had reached £44 3s. 6d., and, after meeting all expenses, there remained £5 3s. in hand.

Mr. Kitson was re-elected hon. secretary and praised for the work he had put in to keep the society going during months of unusual difficulty.—Mr. Edwards was re-elected hon. treasurer and there were no changes in the committee.

Press cutting, Surrey Comet, March 1940

By October 1939 the borough had a list of land to be used for cultivation, though this did not stop their campaign to acquire more. In 1940, 500 posters advertising the need for allotment sites were posted around Surbiton Borough and a loudspeaker van used to broadcast the appeal. By the summer of 1940, they also started targeting the gardens of unoccupied houses.

Alongside gaining all this new land to be managed by the borough, the council also agreed that unlike with the last war, after 31 March 1941 a standard rental fee was to be applied on the plots. This time around, allotments were not going to be free.

In total, the council considered 111 sites across the borough and 48 were selected as wartime allotments covering over 105 acres of land. By 1947 the borough reported that they had 114.520 acres forming 1689 plots. These, together with the permanent allotments and private allotments established for the war effort, meant over 70 sites were cultivated in the war and immediate post-war period.

Even if Surbiton's initial response was strong, the government campaign, originally called 'Grow More Food', did not take off with much enthusiasm owing to a focus on news in Europe, and the so-called "Phoney War" in Britain. On the 6 September a journalist with the Evening Standard, which after his death in 2010 was revealed to be a young Michael Foot, wrote an article in support of the campaign, telling readers "Tell your neighbour and remember yourself that the order is to dig. The spade may prove as mighty as the sword. DIG." On the 12 September in another article by Michael Foot, he used the phrase "Dig for Victory" which was later adopted as the official name of the campaign.

Surrey Comet, 28 Feb 1940

Mr Middleton

Dig for Victory also provided a great deal of support for growers whether it was through official pamphlets, local talks or demonstration plots which Surbiton set up in Victoria Recreation Ground, Alexandra Recreation Ground, King Edward Recreation Ground and at the junction of Chessington Lane and Moor Lane. There were also numerous radio programmes broadcast by the BBC. Of these, the most popular personality by far was that of Mr Middleton. Middleton was a Tolworth resident living at 17 Princes Avenue and was loved for his gentle manner, advice and encouraging words which went down well with the general population. For many he was the voice of Dig for Victory and when he died in September 1945 his contribution to the war effort and funeral from St Matthew's Church, Surbiton was covered by Pathe News in a piece entitled 'The Passing of an Old Friend'.

Local stores, such as Bentalls in Kingston, promoted the campaign to grow more food in the press and selling a wide range of gardening equipment and products. Events were also a help and the Surrey Allotments Council held a meeting at Kew Gardens on 16 July 1944 in response to many requests for such an event and so "...that by meeting socially, the allotment holders can exchange useful experiences of mutual benefit".

The Government introduced growers certificates from the Ministry of Agriculture and a merit scheme with the National Allotment Society. Practical prizes were offered, such as gardening supplies, cash and War Savings Certificates to further incentivise participation in these schemes, especially as there were periodic seed and fertiliser shortages to contend with. To earn the 'Certificate of Merit' Allotment Holders had to prove skills in:

cultivation, management of the compost heap, weed control, rotation of crops, neatness and finish, growth of plants, yield of crops, cleanliness of crops, planning to secure food throughout the year.

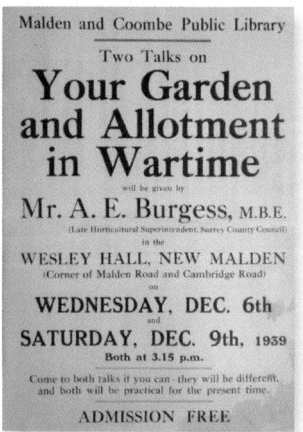

As in 1918, peace did not signal the end to demand for allotments. A 1945 survey by Surbiton Municipal Council found of the 654 participants, 598 wanted a permanent allotment after the war. The waiting lists continued and in 1949 the Surrey Allotment Bulletin claimed that across Surrey, 1,700 people were awaiting an allotment and that more difficulties were being had in the north of the county as there was a high demand on already built-up land. In July 1948, in a response to the Allotments Committee, the secretaries of the Tolworth and District Allotment Holders Society, the Hook Allotment Society and the North Chessington Allotment and Gardens Council set out proposals for existing allotments and layouts of new allotments. They asked the borough to aim for a ratio of 35 plots per 10000 residents. At this time the permanent plot ratio was 15:1000, and when including wartime allotments, the total was 28:1000.

The pressure to rebuild post-war Britain grew and though in 1945 it is thought there were almost 2 million plots in Britain, by the 1970s this had fallen to around 500,000 - back to its 1914 pre-war level.

The Good Life

The second half of the 20th Century saw a great deal of social change. More women were working and the introduction of self-service supermarkets, convenience food and home freezing changed a great deal. This all reduced the necessity of for an allotment, which was still seen by many as a symbol of poverty and a haunting reminder of the austerity of war. The 1960s saw the lowest ever take up of allotments and the government commissioned the *Thorpe Report* to look into the future of the allotment. Though its 44 recommendations were never enacted it had suggested the abandonment of the word "allotment" because of these negative associations with the word, and instead promote the idea that they were a "leisure garden". The British population were increasingly having more time for leisurely pursuits and tapping into this held potential for the resurgence of the allotment.

However, the second half of the 1960s also brought a green revolution and a renewed movement back to the land. There were ever increasing concerns about where food was coming from, how it was being made and the impact this was having on the environment and climate change. Following this, came a surge in people moving to the countryside to become self-sufficient.

Over at the BBC a new sitcom was in development which was looking to explore the idea of the average person's desire to escape their job and follow their dreams, and to do so in a way which would appeal to its audience. In this, the notion of self-sufficiency fit perfectly. Surbiton was chosen as the location, as the name alone projected the idea of the most suburban of areas, and a typical suburban road, The Avenue, was to be home for the characters. Many shows had been made about self-sufficiency, and the writers knew that being self-sufficient in suburbia was all but impossible, so the concept for this show was completely novel. The Good Life had been born.

> "It's absolutely fantastic, obviously we got Mr Middleton, who was the voice for 'Dig for Victory', which is brilliant down in Tolworth. The Good Life, there's a bit of a connection there, everyone thinks of Surbiton and Tolworth with The Good Life."

John Esmonde, Writer, The Good Life

> "The Good Life was to do with doing something with life before it throttles you."

John Esmonde, Writer, The Good Life

What the show's creators were probably unaware of, was that the Surbiton area had encountered a number of trials already when it came to keeping animals on the allotments. In 1915 new rules allowed for applications to keep pigs, although there was initially only one applicant to do so. Mr G E Wall of Egmont Road, was granted permission "subject to his keeping the pigs in such a way as not to be a nuisance". During the Second World War there were numerous applications to keep chickens on plots, but there were also numerous complaints about damage animals caused to the crops. Such as A J.P Luff who in January 1944 was compelled to complain about "...the destruction of the allotments adjoining Green Lane, Chessington, caused by the ducks etc. from "St John's". The Kingston Young Farmers Club were also keen to do their bit, attempting to obtain the allotment land near Buckland Road, Chessington for their use.

One of the many reasons The Good Life was a success was the vastly different personalities self-sufficient Tom and Barbara Good and their middle class and proper neighbours Margo and Jerry Leadbetter. Their friendship was warming and highly entertaining with Margo and Jerry's constant disapproval of their friends' way of life. It is tempting to wonder what Margo and Jerry would have made of the wartime allotments set up on The Avenue, which in December 1943 were described in a complaint as "a little scrappy and half-hearted".

Environmental issues have continued to be a great motivation for the existence and popularity of allotments. The eclectic concentration of plants draws in wildlife and supports biodiversity. Growing food locally reduces the need for food transportation, and encourages recycling, composting and reduction in plastic food packaging. Addison Gardens allotments took composting to a new level and built and opened their own composting toilet in 2011.

Ready for use: Children's author Dame Jacqueline Wilson, sixth left, opens the new composting toilet at Addison Gardens allotments. Deadlinepix KT56728

Going green with loo

A composting toilet has proved popular with curious children and allotment holders alike since being officially opened by Dame Jacqueline Wilson.

The lavatory was unveiled at the Addison Gardens allotment in Kingston on Sunday, April 3.

The children's author said she had been asked to open many buildings before, but a new toilet was a first.

Surrey Comet, 13-19 May 2011

The last 20 years have seen a number of major intitiatives undertaken to ensure the positive environmental impact of allotment land in the area. The first in 1989 saw public opposition to plans by the council to develop half the land of the Tolworth allotments for housing, due to drop in demand for plots. After a strong public petition and consultants concluding the council did not need this land for development, it was decided to create a woodland park instead in order to maintain the much loved green space.

A few years later at the Knollmead Allotments, a disused acre of waterlogged land unsuitable for allotments, was transformed in to the Kingston Permaculture Reserve, now known as Kingston's Edible Forest Garden. It is home to a wide range of trees, shrubs and plants, a tree nursery (growing 21 heritage varieties of apple trees for local schools) and runs fruit growing courses for locals. It has become a site of special biodiversity and cultural value.

Surbiton Fire Station roof allotment

The Heritage Shed at the V&A with oral history participants and supporters

More recently, in 2010, Surbiton firefighter Simon Jakeman was motivated to do his bit for the environment. As a child he had always enjoyed the outdoors and his grandad had an allotment in his garden, but after 23 years of seeing the devastating effects and increased frequency of extreme weather events, he decided to take action. Starting with a tomato plant in a fire bucket, Simon transformed the empty roof terrace on top of Surbiton Fire Station into a garden, providing locally sourced food for the station's mess and a habitat for local wildlife.

As a result, Surbiton was crowned London's greenest Fire Station and Simon became London Fire Brigade's Green Champion of the year, visiting every single watch across London's 103 fire stations to inspire them to start their own projects. Simon has received a host of green awards, 2 RHS medals and was awarded a British Empire Medal in the New Year's honours list in 2017 for services to the environment (Energy and Sustainability).

> "True gardeners never enjoy the fruits of their labours unless they can share them with others"

Mr Middleton, 1945

The Growing Community

Plot holders today will tell you one of the best things about the allotment is the sense of community spirit and support from fellow growers. Historically, allotments and horticulture prompted the formation of a number of friendly societies, community groups and cooperatives. This was usually on a local level and some of the earliest in the area included the Surbiton Horticultural Society which was founded in 1885.

In October 1918 the National Union of Allotment Holders was formed, which by 1930 would merge with other similar groups to form the National Allotment Society. In 1918 in Surbiton, the Tolworth and District Allotment Holders Society was also founded and was one of a number of allotment groups which grew up in the area to support the needs of plot holders and build a sense of community at each site. This Tolworth society had a great resurgence after the Second World War and launched its own magazine, called The Cultivator, in 1948. In its first edition, the Secretary, H. E. Dicker, stated "It is hoped that our very own Monthly "Cultivator" will be the means of helping everyone to make the best use of their garden or allotment." The society also ran sheds for seeds, produce and small tools as well as an annual produce show for many years, but folded in 2014 after 96 years of operation due to lack of sufficient volunteers to form a viable committee and local garden centres offering more competitive prices.

Despite this, many groups still operate, such as the Addison Gardens Allotment Association who state "The purpose of the Association is to promote the growing of fruit and vegetables and also to manage the site to promote a community spirit amongst members and to protect and enhance the environment."

> "I enjoy being over there alone but when people turn up and say 'hello' it's very warming, it's very nice and if I occasionally jump on my bike and just tour round and say hello the either people I know or don't know. There is a very warm friendliness about just stopping admiring what somebody is growing, exchanging names and aims and occasionally people will say 'I just don't seem to be able to grow 'so and so' and if that's something I'm good at I can suggest something and I often offer seed."

Anna Cunnyngham

Societies have played an important role too in creating social cohesion through produce shows with the produce exhibited traditionally given away to charity as many allotment societies view the sale of produce as going against the spirit of the allotment and grounds for expulsion. The shows were highly important in wartime too, and **Mr Middleton** promoted them as he believed they kept societies motivated and active, which was true even in peacetime.

The allotment has also been used as a tool for inclusion. In June 1916, Surrey's County War Agricultural Committee asked for Belgian soldiers in Surbiton to be found allotment plots and the council promised to try and accommodate them at Tolworth. This was just one of the many ways in which the local area were trying to support some of the many Belgian's who had sought refuge in the wider Kingston area. Local people pledged money to run two hostels in Kingston to house the refugees, and a fundraising exhibition of Belgian artists was held at Kingston Museum in 1915 for the same cause.

However, by 1919 not everyone was feeling quite as welcome to the allotment community. Despite a national movement to give demobilised soldiers plots to ease their transition back to a normal life, a complaint was made to Surbiton Urban District Council by the local branch of the National Federation of Discharges and Demobilised Soldiers. They reported that a soldier had made a complaint, saying he did not feel he was being treated fairly with his application for a permanent allotment, and that preference was being given to civilians who had not served.

Yet, if an example of how growing brought communities together was ever needed, most would argue that the Dig for Victory campaign was just that. In 1942, the beloved **Mr Middleton** declared "...let us all work together to make this the greatest and most successful gardening year we have ever had. Let us break down the barriers of exclusiveness and be good neighbours, and help each other all we can".

Though wartime spirit was strong, it was not unanimous and complaints made their way to the council offices. Despite trespass on allotments being a statutory offence, vandalism and theft was rife and damaging the spirit of the plot holders.

A letter in October 1943 from a Miss M E Batchelor, who had a plot on Raeburn Road, outlined her feelings to the council perfectly.

"I should like to draw your attention once more to the wilful petty damage and pilfering which continues to take place on these allotments...it is very disheartening to have one's plants and other growing vegetables uprooted just when you are about to harvest them, only last week a pumpkin weighing about 8lbs. was torn right off the vine and it's hopeless to plant leeks, they are just pulled out and left lying round, we are asked by the Government to grow all we can, but it is not very encouraging to find all the work and time (what spare most of us have after a days work in Town) only to have it all destroyed."

Borough of Surbiton.

Defence (General) Regulations, 1939.

TAKE NOTICE that any person found trespassing on these allotments is guilty of an offence against Regulation 61 (2) of the above Regulations and is liable on summary conviction to a fine not exceeding £50.

R. H. WRIGHT,
Town Clerk.

Children were often believed to be the perpetrators in these cases and in 1946 headteachers of schools in the borough were asked to give talks to their students on the subject of allotment damage. This was paired with notices in the press, appeals at Town Council meetings and working alongside the police, all to help prevent damage on the allotment sites.

In August 1946 Lieutenant Col W E Shaw (retired) wrote to the council regarding a break in to his property at 28 Ewell Road where many items from his house were stolen, he believed that access had been obtained via a path used to access the Romsey Lodge allotment site, where he had no gate as it was taken for war purposes. Shaw used the opportunity to express that while he had no complaints against the plot holders themselves, he did notice that while he was away on holiday, they had taken fruit from his garden, and used his outside lavatory.

Plot holders also had to contend with enemy action. There were at least eight air raids which resulted in bombs falling on allotments, four of which in 1940/41 are recorded as having caused no damage, and four in 1944 which were all unexploded. However, for R H Owen who had a plot at the Alexandra Recreation Ground where a bomb fell on 23 February 1944, his problem was not with the device, but with the hole the Disposal Squad left in his plot after removing the bomb.

Surprisingly, it was also the success of growing in the wartime allotments which created a different social movement, as in some areas in Britain there was a surplus of food which needed managing. The Women's Institute stepped in to help, and along with the National Allotment Society, councils and horticultural societies redistributed excess food through the greengrocery trade running over 5,800 Preservation Centres across the country, where they filled jars, cans and bottles ready for market and to be donated to hospitals and schools.

The produce from the demonstration plots were also put to good use, such as to Surbiton Hospital who were sent 60 lbs of potatoes, 15 lbs of marrows, 10lbs of beetroots and 25lbs of carrots in 1941. Also that year the Soldiers', Sailors' & Airmans' Families Association contacted the Head Groundsman at Alexandra Recreation Ground asking whether they could spare a few items a week from their Exhibition Allotment for families in need.

In more recent years, the community has once again stepped in to take an active interest in the management of allotment sites, and more power has been passed to such groups, with local authorities and landowners playing less active roles in their management. In July 2003 the Kingston Federation of Allotment Gardeners (KFAG) was formally established in order to provide a forum to liaise with the council and to help let unused plots. KFAG promotes allotment gardening across the modern day borough, provides information, support and advice to sites considering voluntary management of their allotments, and builds relationships within and between the allotment sites. In 2008 the Royal Borough of Kingston upon Thames released a 10 year strategy, with input from KFAG, to improve allotment provision and management with input from plot holders and associations. That same year, KFAG negotiated with the council a 'model' lease for new voluntary managed sites and for lease renewals at existing voluntary managed sites.

It is clear that pressures on land use and change in the law and public policy have impacted on the area of land open to public use for growing.

'Traditionally when people think about planning and development they're thinking about starting with the big picture, starting at the top and looking downwards and that doesn't work unless somebody is starting at the bottom and looking sideways because you can plan too easily for a town without planning life into it. Life doesn't come from planners, life comes from people who live there. The vital thing about SHEDx is that it is exciting the people who already live in the place to find more potential in where they live, more links to each other, more ways to resist some of the things that are happening cotemporally that they don't like. More ways of greening the town all of which is just to do with infusing life into the town which we've got to have as well as making some structural changes to the town.'

Bob Phillips

Change of Land Use

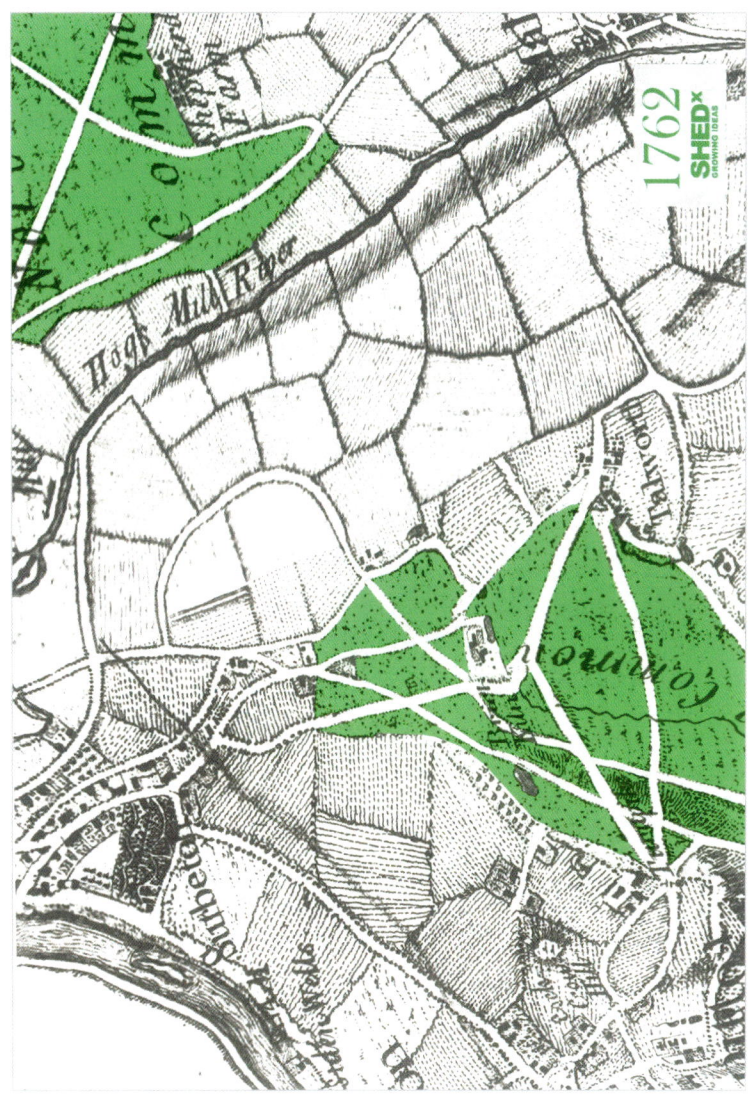

Allotment map – 1762

Until the Victorian period, a large part of the countryside in Britain was "Common Land".

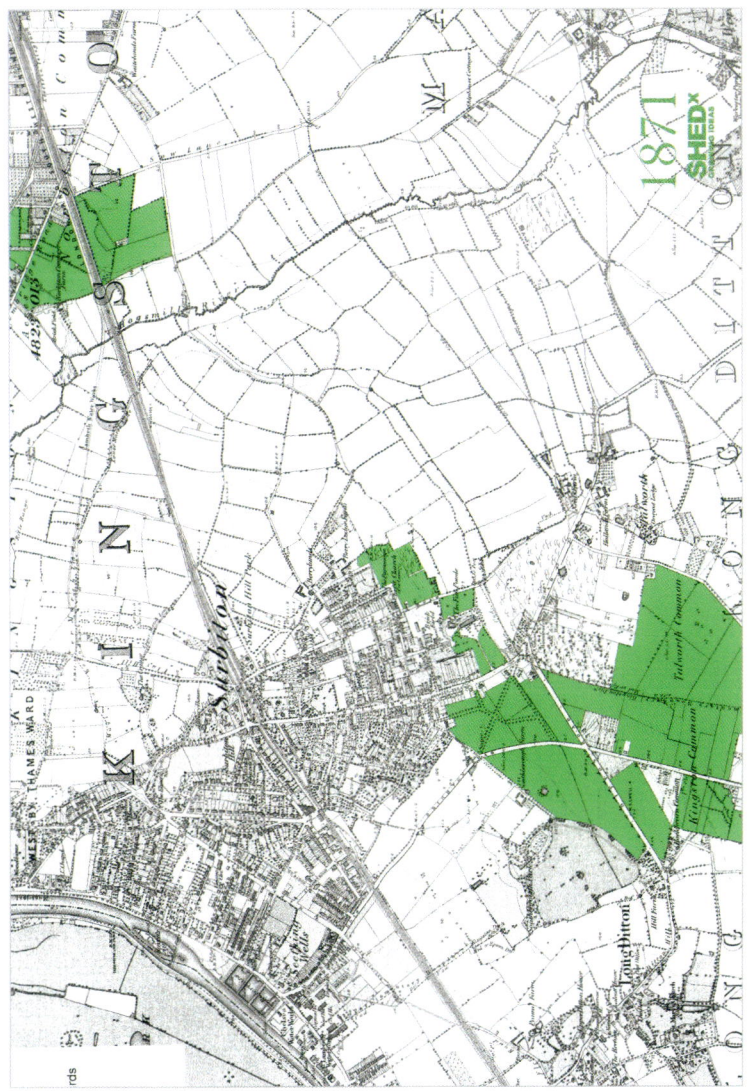

Allotment map – 1871

Things changed dramatically with the enclosure movement. This sought to divide the countryside into the larger fenced fields we would recognise today.

Allotment map – 1910

Farm owners could not afford to increase the wages they paid to their workers. The only way they could help was to give the workers pieces of unused land so they could grow their own food.

Allotment map – 1940

During World War II, plans were made for food rationing and the campaign to grow food at home started again.

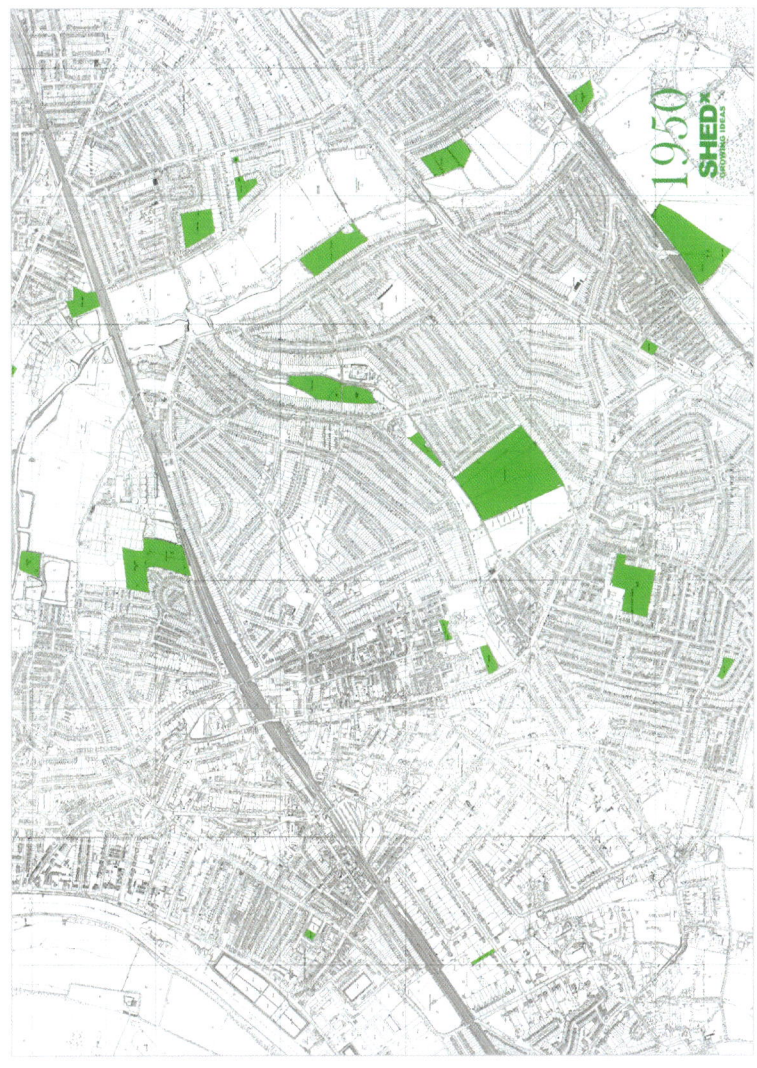

Allotment map – 1950

This map from 1950 depicts the true legacy that the government's Dig for Victory had in the local area. Allotment space had been greatly increased in the Borough and it wasn't until the latter part the 20th Century that allotment space decreased.

Allotment map – 2018

In 2018 there were 22 allotment sites made up of 1,200 plots in Kingston Borough.

Original shed for heritage shed recreation

> "The shed, with all its expression of individuality, can take pride of place on the plot."

Crouch and Ward, 1997

The Shed

The wonderful community spirit found on allotments does not detract from the fact that each plot is its own kingdom and sanctuary, full of individual expression and character. Part of its identity is the shed.

Many allotment sheds are home-made, inherited from plot owners before them or perhaps re-used with an entirely different former purpose. There aren't many controls on the allotment shed, but by-laws generally control the location and erection of them, so as to maintain some control over the layout of the allotment site.

This was the case in Surbiton and the council were strict in adherence to the rules, with sheds being ordered to be moved or dismantled if illegally put up. These were the conditions issued by the Borough Surveyor in 1940 with regards to application for a shed in Raeburn Avenue:

1. Size shall not exceed 5'x4'x7' high

2. The shed is to be placed at the bottom of your allotment next to the existing hedge

3. The shed is to be well built and creosoted brown or green

4. The shed is to be maintained in a good condition and to my satisfaction

5. The shed is to be used only for the storage of garden tools, materials and appliances

However, as the war progressed, the shortage of materials for sheds caused problems for the Hook Allotment Association based at King Edward Recreation Ground. They were granted permission for a tool shed in 1941 but the council could not gift materials, so instead permitted use of material salvaged from bomb sites so they got their "new" store in 1943. At the end of the war, with continued shortages, the Vacation Committee notified all allotment holders that Anderson Shelters on the allotment sites could be used as tool sheds. Still in 1948 Tolworth and District Allotment Holders Society were unable to obtain wood and so erected an Anderson Shelters with brick ends for a shed instead.

After the war, the council also tried to adopt a policy of supplying and erecting standard sheds on allotment sites for a charge rather than granting permission for individual sheds. The plan was detailed in trade press and in a reply to a Horticultural Instructor from Reading who enquired as to what these sheds would be like, the Borough Surveyor explained "...the sheds consist in the main of Anderson Shelter parts with brick filling at each end. Bricks being used are those salvaged from the demolition of A.R.P shelters; the base in concrete". He went on to say that though a decision on how the huts would be erected had not yet been made, it was hoped that there would be assistance from the various allotment associations.

As part of the 'SHEDx – Grow for Good' project MA Architecture students (MArch Unit 5) from Kingston University, under the tutorage of Takeshi Hayatsu and Jim Reed, worked with volunteers and allotment holders to record some of the sheds on the Tolworth Main Allotment. The project was particularly interested in those sheds that had been hand built (rather than flat pack assembly). It is clear that the number of bespoke sheds is reducing in the light of cheaper mass-produced models.

Alexia

Ziad

Britt

Rosie

Rohith

Verity

Darren

Maija

Austin

Gemma

Alex

Salah

Serina

Elle

Ben

Dan

Jason

Matt

Youjin

Arjun

One of these sheds was chosen to be recreated as an exact replica that could be taken 'on tour' to different venues both within the borough of Kingston and beyond. It has visited over ten different venues including being on display in the courtyard of the Victoria and Albert Museum and the forecourt of The Garden Museum at Lambeth Palace. The Heritage Shed, with accompanying allotment went to the Hampton Court Flower Show in 2018 winning a silver medal and returned in 2019 with a new mixed allotment and won the top 'Five Flowers' Award.

At all of the venues where it appears the shed contains recordings of oral histories of local allotment holders. You can read some of their stories later in this book as well as other personal tales of local allotment holding.

“ We are interested in production and its empowering nature for local communities. Unit 5 is focused on the craft of building. ”

Statement from the Unit 5 students

The Heritage Shed

The following is from Unit 5 – MA Architecture students from Kingston University who participated in the project from the beginning.

Unit 5's year started at Tolworth Allotments, where we collaborated with The Community Brain and the residents of the allotments to capture their plots and create a lasting legacy which celebrates locally produced food and the allotments shared heritage. Our contribution is multi-faceted and it is envisaged that this project will be a catalyst for a long and meaningful relationship between the department of architecture and the community in which the university resides. Through careful analysis, each student has aimed to capture their plots history, character, narrative and the person behind its growth through a series of drawings showing plans, elevations, an axonomentric, photos and a section. This has created a unique collection of drawings across the unit which shows our understanding of the allotment and its people.

This was supported by the Unit's collective research on the Tolworth allotment movement, further supported by a field trip to Berlin where we visited several community allotments: The Prinzessinnengarten, Templehof Airport and the Gärtnerei Berlin – all of which have provided inspiration to the students and our allotment project.

As part of our own analysis, we collaborated with The Community Brain, volunteers and allotment holders to recreate our selected heritage shed. Working together as a team, we have designed, detailed and constructed the recreation of the shed which has presented its challenges but ultimately has been an incredibly rewarding experience; one which has aided our expertise in craft and construction. This project has been a catalyst for our thesis project where we are looking to echo the focus on production and design within a suburban context.

The original shed

Situated at the front of Tolworth Allotment, the original shed sits greeting all visitors to the site. Cobbled together with found timber, the shed represents a time before the days of the 'flat pack' shed; which many of its distinctive features signify. Amongst many others, perhaps its most striking feature is its 'wonk' and its beautiful decorative panels covering its West elevation. The shed was surveyed meticulously by students in Unit 5 to ensure all of its features were recorded in order to replicate its 'recreation' and ensure that its characteristics were accurately embodied for the SHEDx heritage project.

The heritage shed then went on tour to a number of venues both within Tolworth and other areas of the borough and to the V&A museum, Hampton Court Garden Festival and The Garden Museum at Lambeth.

Inside the shed were illustrations of other sheds from the Tolworth Main Allotments and oral histories recorded during the project were played. These featured local residents talking about their memories of their allotments and the importance of growing to them.

Volunteers from the project helped to tour the shed and staff it as well as helping to grow and plant the display for the RHS show.

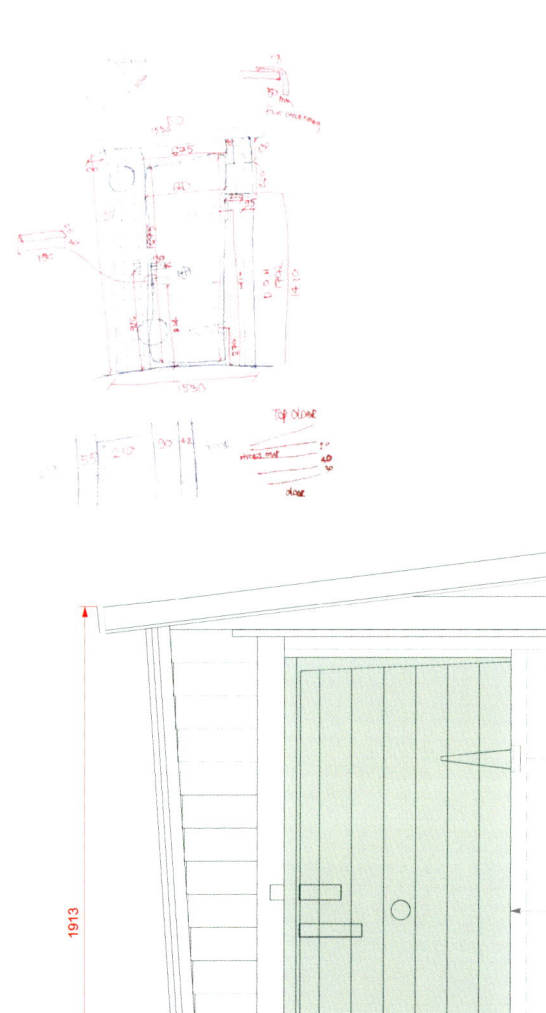

Door as an individual slot-in element

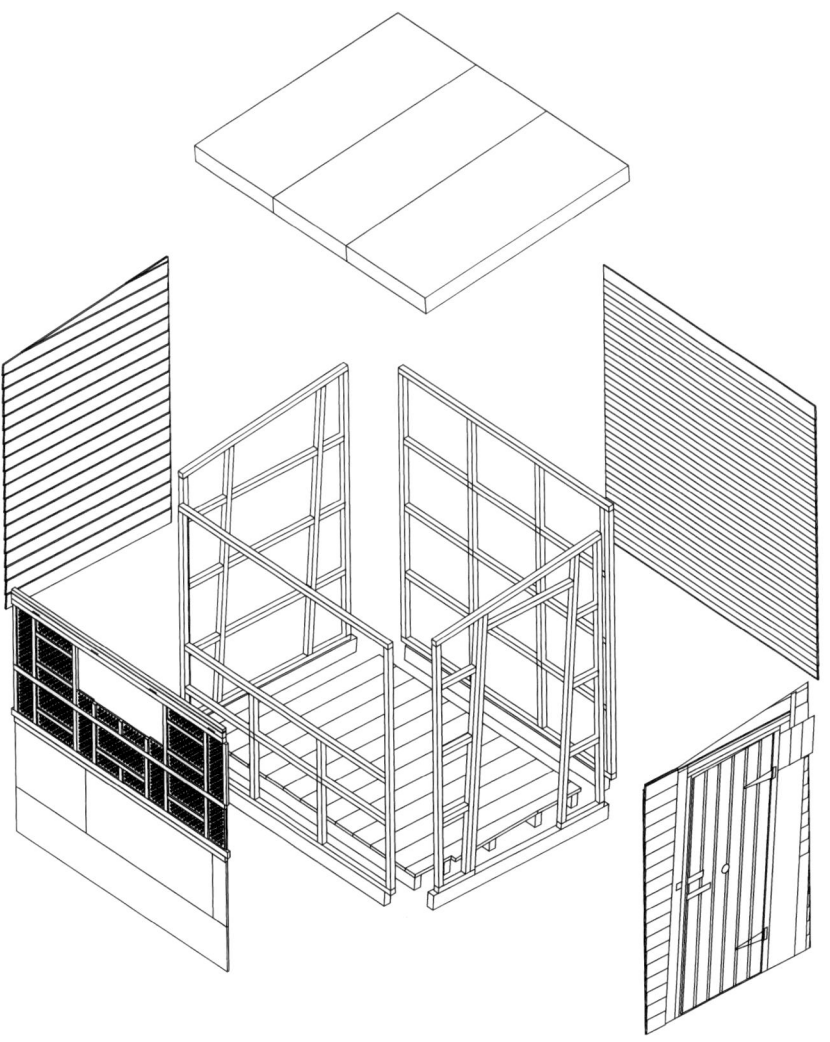

Unit 5 – MA Architecture students from Kingston University construct the heritage shed

Heritage shed at the V&A

Hampton Court

Hampton Court

The Garden Museum

Allotment Holders Tales

from the 'SHEDx - Grow for Good' Oral Histories

Julia Dennis and Kathy Munnings

What is your relationship to this allotment?

I grew up in Yorkshire and when I was a child we would grow food in our gardens if the farmers could not provide us with the things we needed like turnips or onions we just did not have it. So I was taught how to garden at a very early age. I like to set myself a task everyday, if I complete the task I am happy, but if I start to get a horrible pain then I take it easy. It is a never ending process. It is a lot of work, and I think what a lot of people make the mistake with is they will do two days digging up the allotment, two to three weeks later the weeds are all grown back, you can see over there, I did those weeds a week ago and they are right back, so that's how quickly the weeds have grown. If people neglect their plots and allow the weeds to grow we all suffer, because the seeds will blow and everyone will be affected. Everyone here knows each other and we help each other as much as we can.

What are these water bottles on a stick for?

When the wind blows it makes a rattling noise, and what this does is create a disturbance to the pigeons, I don't have anything on them but they are a nuisance sometimes. There are different methods like using blank CDs which reflect light and that causes somewhat of a distraction however I find this method best.

How long have you been at the allotments for?

11 years roughly. I moved here 11 years ago and I more or less had one straight away.

What were the first impressions and coming into the allotment community like?

At first, I was rather anxious about coming into this community. Some people have had their allotments for 40, even 50 years, and in all honesty, at the beginning I felt intimidated. Before owning an allotment, I assumed that it is mainly for older people to potter around in, but was proven completely otherwise.

Immediately, I was drawn to the shed, even though at the time was quite run down, dirty and left in an old wood looking condition. The plot itself was overgrown with weeds up to the waist when I first arrived, so you could see only a part of the shed. Getting involved with gardening gave me motivation to get out of the house, and the feeling of achievement with each days' worth of work was overwhelmingly rewarding.

Shed owners, Kathy Munnings and Julia Dennis

One of the main features that drew me to your plot was the striking colour palette. Could you talk a little about the beautiful colours you chose?

Purple is one of my favourite colours, and I love the film 'The Colour Purple' which is so moving and powerful, which means that to me, this colour bears a strong connotation to being powerful and strong. It was an encouragement for me to be strong.

I didn't realise originally how large your allotment plot is! How do you keep up its maintenance?

This plot is 100 square metres. You see we work 'crop rotation', so we have cabbage there, potatoes here and beans. Those things are growing wild in there now. You rotate them yearly so nothing grows in the same place for four years. Its called soil management. Everything you buy in the supermarket is grown in these super big greenhouses and nothings fresh like this here.

How old is your grape vine?

Around the 1920's I reckon, a nice lady on another plot asked if I wanted it and so I took it and its been on my plot ever since."

Do you often get those foxes (appearing from behind the shed) visiting your plot?

I've had a pheasant walking around here as well. The annoying thing is now they've built their den here, so I'm going to have blinking fox cubs, they're like kittens, they're barmy! They're babies they have to learn, I've tried to stop the lads in the yard feeding them so that they learn to hunt like they need to be able to do in the wild...the Pigeons around here will want to stay out the way now.

Simon Jakeman

We got our own allotment. We've had it in Hook since 2010. It was first from a conversation of neighbours. And we said we must do something, start growing some of our own food, getting the children involved. So it was one cold night - winter's night and we thought let's do it. So put our name down for an allotment, long waiting list down at Hook. But they actually decided to open up part of the allotment what hadn't been used for a very long time so it was all overgrown.

So we went down, had a look - and it really was overgrown. 120 foot allotment, probably 20 foot high brambles. Bits and pieces, we had to cut our way in. That's how it started and then we started clearing it slowly, preparing the ground so that was back 2010 and we got everyone involved. It was family, friends, neighbours. All ages. Our youngest was 3 at the time. And the eldest was in their 80s. So yes we all got down there. Started clearing a bit - we done a lot of the hard work and then yeah. We started building raised beds, greenhouses. Someone had donated us a greenhouse. Local greenhouse what we carried down there. Couple of sheds. Yeah, just superb. So, 2010. That's when we started.

And the fact that it was totally overgrown didn't deter you?

Not at all, it was more of a challenge. It would have been lovely if it was ready to go as an allotment that you - y'know picture in a book. But it was great because it was like a blank canvas so we could do whatever we wanted to do then. There was brambles, huge brambles. I don't know how long this part of the allotment had been empty, it was a big challenge. So it probably took good six months just to get it cleared more than anything. But we started growing straight away, that's somewhere - I think it was just potatoes to start off with. But yeah we had we had a few barbecues and that kind of thing, there was 30 or 40 of us down there one day and we just blitzed it. So yeah. Fantastic.

So it's more of a community, more people involved than just yourself and the family.

Yeah it started off like that because of neighbours. I think there was about five or six families and then we got our children's friend's families involved as well. And the idea was erm we noticed that so many of the children were just plugged in, they're not out playing, that kind of thing. So we just wanted to get them outside and we thought if they could start learning where food comes from, what it looks like, rather than it being in a supermarket then they might - some birds and butterflies, and insects. What's that, that kind of thing. Just get them outside.

And how did the children react to this?

Yeah really good, they really enjoyed being outside and just y'know. Getting in the mud and digging. And some of them were really young but they were so helpful and yeah brilliant. We even had a few posters - we had one of the sheds, we turned that into a sort of like a main hub so we had an old desk. We had all the children paint the desk and they put butterflies and flowers on it and activities that kind of thing. Just to get them involved and even our - our sign, our number on our allotment we had the children painting that, we've still got that there. And that's 8 years ago now. So yeah really good. Just-just brilliant.

And have you managed to keep the children and other people involved the allotment or has it sort of gravitated to just one or two people?

Yeah there's a few that have slowly disappeared as there always is. But we always have at least three days where everyone turns so it's - everyone turns up so we have an event in March time what we call the Great Big Earth Dig. And we made posters, we've even got a website just for us really and then we take photos of everyone and that kind of thing. So that's spring. Then usually sort of round Father's Day we manage to get everyone up there sort of June time, for a bit of a weed and tidy up, that kind of stuff. And then harvest time - so we try and do Halloween, have a bit of a bonfire and get everyone up for Halloween and a bit of another tidy up. So that's the main things - main three days.

And the children still talking about it now, they're all teenagers now but they still love the allotment and talk about the days they've had down there so hopefully we planted that seed for when they're older, then they'll pass it onto their next generation. That's what it was all about. Where it started for me was my - my grandad had an allotment. What was absolutely fantastic and then he actually moved further away. He moved to Gloucestershire so he could have a bigger garden, so he could have his allotment in his garden and the whole garden was able to grow food. I still remember the smell of his greenhouse. I still love watering tomatoes. It just reminds me of my grandad's garden. It's just brilliant, yeah, so that's where it comes from. Erm. Dig for Victory. I suppose, he was World War Two. Dig For Victory, where everyone was growing and that's where his idea – self-sufficiency of, well doing their bit.

So whilst - whilst you've got your grandfather's legacy. Was 2010 the first time that you personally started growing food?

Yeah it's probably around - just before 2010, being a - being a firefighter, being on the front line of climate change, that seed what was planted when I was a child suddenly popped into my head. Erm. Being a firefighter, being out in the climate, you know front line of climate change, floods, wildfires, storms. I started thinking about - well we've got to try to do something about it. So if we could start growing our own food, locally sourced food. It's not coming from the other side of the world. So that's how it sort of started. So we got our allotment and then I took it to the fire station and that started with one fire bucket up on the roof with one tomato plant. And that's when we thought well we're grow some tomatoes for our mess in the fire station. And everyone realised by growing those tomatoes how great they tasted. Everyone thought they were just getting older and tomatoes didn't taste of - they just taste of water. But that's because they come for so far, been frozen or whatever they done. You eat a tomato straight off the plant, it's just the best thing in the world.

Simon Jakeman

Surbiton Fire Station, do they grow their own food?

Yes so it started off with that fire bucket. Erm up on the roof, it's a flat roof, there used to be - the station manager used to live there with their own family. So it's like a balcony kind of terrace garden. So it started off with that one fire bucket. We got permission to grow the tomatoes and to clear a garden. So we've cleared it - it was just covered in moss. There's the whole allotment up there now. We grow potatoes, leeks. What else is there. There's kale up there - cauliflower. There's fruit trees up there. Everything just goes into the kitchen, into the mess. Everyone can help themselves. We grew enough food for Christmas dinner. Sprouts from up on the roof. It's on the back of the fire station but it's just an oasis. With all that concrete everywhere. It was just a concrete box before. There's wildflowers up there. There's bird boxes, there's bug boxes.

What was the sort of feedback from the other firefighters?

So at first they asked what are you up to? What are you doing, why are we doing this? A few got a few involved and then everyone's realised how great it is. People have brought different plants in as well. We've got a water feature up there as well now. Obviously we've got more important things to do than gardening. But it's great for health and wellbeing. We've even got a mindfulness in London Fire Brigade what's in Brixton. So where it started off - one fire station, it started spreading out. New Malden Fire Station have got a wildlife garden. Kingston Fire Station looking at doing a community garden and maybe growing some vegetables with local schools. But it's spread across the whole of London Fire Brigade so everyone's now growing their own food. Yeah it-it's just fantastic. It's amazing that one step has just gone off all directions. Yeah, fantastic.

Ray Eades

Ray Eades is one of the longest serving plot holders in the Kingston borough, having held an allotment on Tolworth Main for over 30 years.

Well I first took an allotment at Tolworth about yes 1983. Thereabouts. My allotment at that time was behind the Surbiton British Legion and Surbiton Town Bowling Club, their pavilions. And was the site of the original allotments at Tolworth. But that site now is what is known as the Millennium Ground and there's no longer any allotments there. But I had the advantage of getting the grass cuttings if I needed them from the bowling greens - they would very nicely dumped just outside the gate right by my allotment at that time. But it was double edged sword because if you got cuttings at the wrong time when weed killer had been put on you wouldn't want that on your plot or too much in the compost so. It was a thing we had to just take care of. I can remember my plot number there was Plot Number 50. And my neighbour I had at that time also as it turned out was chap living in the same road as myself. Quite by chance, our plots were adjoining and he is no longer with us, long since gone. But as gardener he was absolutely first class, he would grow the most magnificent vegetables.

Martin Ursell

Over 20 years on the Tolworth Main allotment site Martin Ursell has witnessed many changes - from the development of the Millennium Green to the broadening of his own palette through exotic vegetables introduced to him by neighbouring plot holders.

Everybody down there is very friendly - it's always been like that. And one of the changes is a lot of different cultures and nationalities . When I first had that plot there wasn't but now we have people from all of the world really who have a plot. Two of my neighbours are from Hong Kong. And they have introduced onto the allotment these Chinese vegetables. They started off with something called yau mak choi, which is actually from Taiwan, not Hong Kong, but it's absolutely delicious. It's a wheat derivative that looks a little bit like a long narrow spinach, but it's actually wheat - it's absolutely delicious. I would say a third of that allotment are growing that now. And then they've just started with another one called ong choi which is a hollow stemmed leafy vegetable and that needs a hot year.

Gloria Wallis

In her dual roles as secretary of the Beverly Park allotment site in New Malden and secretary of the Kingston Federation of Allotment Gardeners (KFAG), as well as being a plot holder herself for 34 years, Gloria Wallis has witnessed a great number of changes in the culture and organisation of allotment gardening. Demographics have changed since her time as a rare female presence to the present day, where around half the plots are occupied by women.

Once we got the women in things changed a lot. Before- when I first took my plot on it was mostly men that had allotments. I was in my late 30s then and I pitched up, started an allotment. And they looked me up and down and as you can see I'm not very big and they used to be 'will hubby be helping you?' And I say 'I jolly well hope not, he's no gardener you know' and I think they thought she won't last five minutes. I had my daughter with me who was about 4 at the time and she was moaning and groaning and whining cos the grass was scratching her legs and it was hot and - so I was carrying her. And I heard one of these old boys who were showing me around saying - he was probably a bit younger than I am now - saying to another one 'she must be stronger than she looks y'know. She's carrying that kid all round.'

Joan McConn

As chair of the Kingston Federation of Allotment Gardeners (KFAG) which she helped establish twelve years ago, Joan McConn has memories of her father's allotment while growing up in Liverpool and her own history with owning a plot on Addison Gardens where she grows a wide variety of vegetables

I like being out at doors. I've always wanted to do something practical. I was working up in Westminster in office based jobs, always office based jobs. And I just wanted to be out at doors. So that's why I come home, put my jeans on and go to the allotment. So it was partly pleasure but also the enjoyment of growing stuff really. And I liked experimenting, trying to grow new ones and my husband's the same. So he grows all sorts of weird and wonderful potatoes. Oh I was runner up in the Potato Brain of Great Britain once, and it sounds very impressive but it wasn't. I belong to Garden Organic for - I think I joined in 1988. And Garden Organic used to be called the Henry Doubleday Research Association, it's based in Ryton in the Midlands. And their remit was to encourage people to grow organically before it became fashionable.

Bob Phillips - Allotment holder and volunteer

The shed represents in a sort of shambolic British way everything about the allotment culture and the allotment culture is a profoundly iconic part of what being British is all about and its particularly important now with everyone understanding how important the natural environment is. But it seems to me what was being celebrated with the shed and also all the oral histories that went with the shed is a long, long history of ordinary people taking pieces of land that aren't worth a huge amount of money can be sort of rested away from the developers and the councillors and doing personal, important and environmental things with it and it's been going on for years and years, generations and generations and it's not planned and it's not systematic and it's not pre-fabricated and the shed is a fabulous symbol for that.

Anna Cunnyngham - Allotment holder and volunteer

I was a war time baby and by the time I was conscious of gardens we'd moved back to the London house and the end third of the garden was my Father's vegetable garden and we had apple trees and a plum tree, and gooseberries and currents beside the bean row and the lettuce you know it was all there when I was a small child in fact he had to restrain us all, us kids, the three of us from going down there and raiding his vegetables.

Salah Krichen - Unit 5 Kingston University and volunteer

It was a very bizarre feeling. I have to say when we were first doing the project I don't think any of the students or tutors probably would have ever imagined it to be at the V&A against that red wall. And so it was just an amazing experience and it was amazing to see people's reactions not just at the V&A but even at the University, Flower Shows etc, the smile that it brought on people's faces and kind of curious, made people curious to see what it was about.

Keith McMahon - Allotment Holder and volunteer

I learnt about whether allotments were self-managed or managed by the local authority. I discovered people took on allotments from their parents, from their grandparents so there was this continuity within a family being passed down so there was heritage being built as we watched. People coming back and saying, 'Oh I didn't remember this, or I didn't remember that' and it was nice to be able to prompt people to understand what they had enjoyed over the years.

As mentioned at the beginning of this book 'SHEDx – Grow for Good' was the genesis for a larger project 'SHEDx – Growing Ideas in Tolworth'. It is a project supported by the Mayor of London's Good Growth Fund designed to stimulate communities in Tolworth, and surrounding areas, to become engaged in re-imagining space, both urban and green, through interventions and creative opportunities.

SHEDx is an opportunity to deliver community-led regeneration amidst larger scale transformation as the area prepares to undergo major changes in the coming years. The project takes its inspiration from the humble British allotment shed, in a programme where communities and individuals gather to share ideas and skills, sparking initiatives that will have a wider benefit for their local area.

Work to date has included:

- Teaching food growing, piloting aquaponics, the creation of mobile green seed pod sheds to stimulate new planting area.
- The lifting of the lids on some poorly designed benches on Tolworth Broadway to create new planters to support wildlife and better air quality.
- Adopting Tolworth Railway Station and holding events and markets and encouraging better knowledge and enjoyment of the areas green spaces.
- Designing new benches and planters for cycle routes and to encourage walking.

The photos on the following pages show just some of this work.

You can find out more at SHEDx.org

Tolworth Tower community engagement event

Volunteers prepare the ground for a heritage allotment

Adopting Tolworth Station

Green seed pods

Benches before and as planters

New benches at New Malden 'Go Cycle' scheme

'First Seen in Tolworth' market

The Community Brain is a community interest company which exists to develop community cohesion using the widest range of the arts, education and local history in order to give people and place renewed importance and pride.

The Community Brain is about utilising people's natural talents and energies to develop stronger communities and relationships. It is about strengthening the natural networking and support that can happen in healthy societies creating more resilient communities. It is about believing everyone is brilliant if they are given the help and support.

At the heart of all of our work are stories. Who tells the story of your life? How can we create the stories that celebrate our communities and where we live, work or study? How do you re-imagine and curate your own future story?

We also have a never-ending passion for laughter and play. Many of our community projects start in a place of discovery through smiling, feeling like you are back in the playground, learning about ourselves and others through enjoying our lives and the time and space we share.

You can find out more at our website thecommunitybrain.org

The National Lottery Heritage Fund is the largest dedicated funder of heritage in the UK.

We believe that understanding, valuing and sharing our heritage brings people together, inspires pride in communities and boosts investment in local economies.

We distribute National Lottery grants from £3,000 to £5million and over, funding projects that sustain and transform the UK's heritage

We provide leadership and support across the heritage sector, and advocate for the value of heritage

You can find out more about their work at heritagefund.org.uk

Contributors

Alban Low

Alex Beard

Alex Fedyk

Alexia Alvarez Reyes

Aniela Zaba

Anna Cunnyngham

Arjun Singh

Austin Stapleton

Ben Tynegate

Bob Phillips

Britt Crayston

Charlotte Levy

Dan Rooke

Darren Maskell

Elle Bytautaite

Gavin Blann

Gemma Thompson

Georgia Neesham

Gillian Butler

Glen Rowden

Gloria Wallis

Jarek Zaba

Jason Jennings

Jim Reed

Joan McConn

Julia Dennis

Kathy Munnings

Keith McMahon

Leslie Green

Lionel Randall

Maija Pajanen

Marianne Green

Martin Ursell

Matt Wynn

Pablo Feito Boirac

Pamela Lawson

Ray Eades

Rohith Kakkoprath Edayilveedu

Rosie Cheng

Salah Krichen

Serina Herb

Simon Jakeman

Stephen Simpson

Takeshi Hayatsu

Youjin Cui

Ziad Bakr

With thanks to

The National Lottery Heritage Fund

Kingston University

The Mayor of London

The Royal Borough of Kingston upon Thames

The Community Brain volunteers

The Allotment Holders of Tolworth, Surbiton and Chessington

The RHS

The V&A

The Garden Museum

The Rose Theatre

The Kingston History Centre

Kingston First

Corinthian-Casuals Football Club

Court Farm Garden Centre

Hayatsu Architects

Reed Watts Architects

South Western Railways

121 Collective

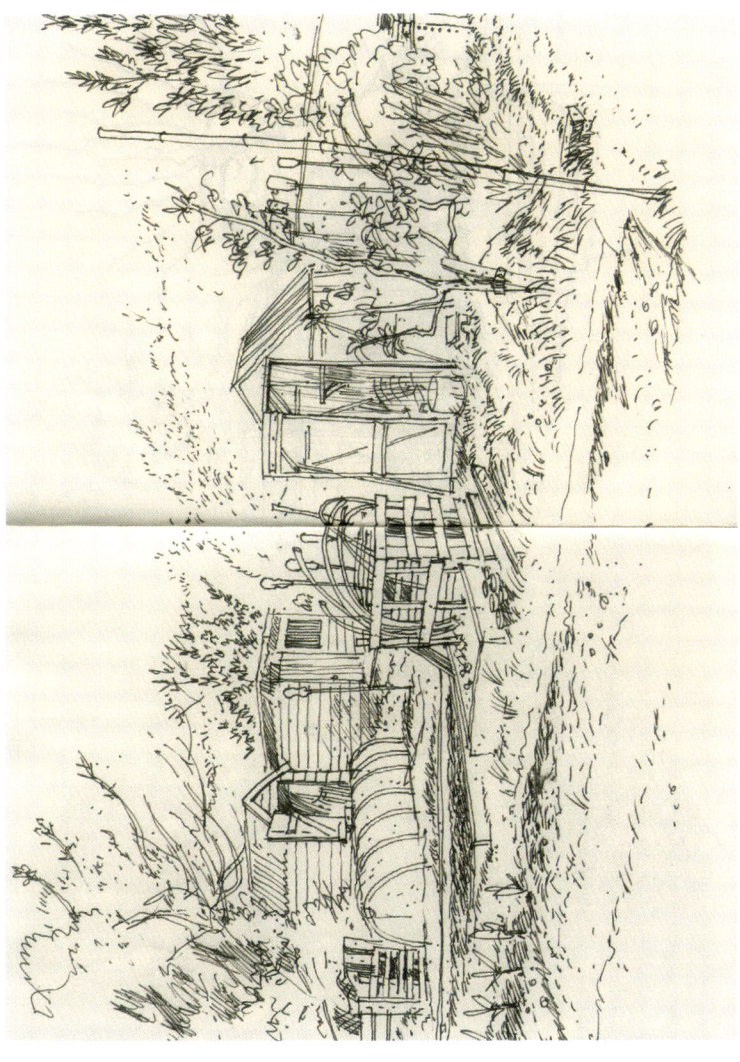

Illustrations by Martin Ursell, Tolworth Main Allotments Holder

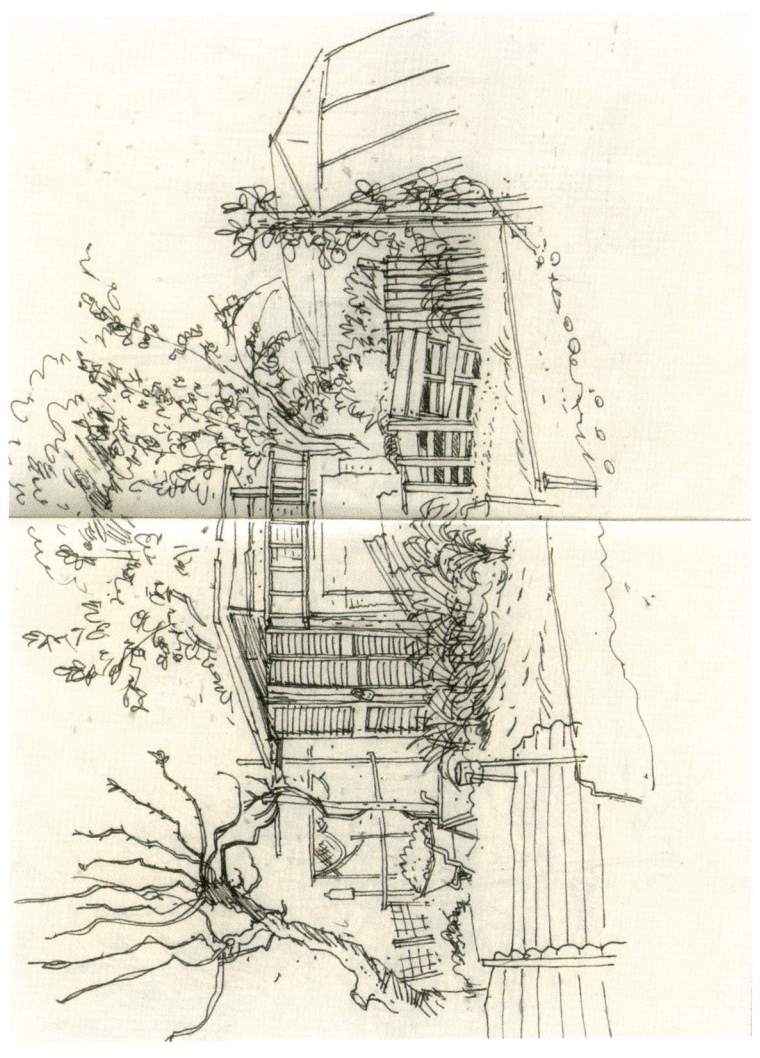

Illustrations by Martin Ursell, Tolworth Main Allotments Holder